Liang Style

Baguazhang

Forms and Martial Applications

by Wang Zhang Yuan

Baguazhang or «**The Palm of Eight trigrams**» it is one of main schools of traditional **Chinese Wushu** of the **internal** branch, which founder is considered as a famous fighter of the past **Dong Haichuan**. Being a marvelous teacher, he educated a whole pleiad of talented pupils, each of which continued the business of their teacher and created own style, introducing certain corrections and nuances in the techniques.

The book, offered to readers' attention step by step presents methods, practices and techniques of the martial art of "Eight trigrams", originated from **Liang Zhenpu**, who was one of most famous teachers of the school.

© 2018, Dudukchan I.M.
All Rights reserved.
Author: Wang Zhang Yuan
Translator: Elena Novitskaja
ISBN: 9781730946974

Contents:

Introduction...4
Chapter 1
The brief biography of Baguazhang Liang style
masters...10
Chapter 2
 Base principles of Baguazhang.................................14
Chapter 3
Ding Shi Ba Zhang – «Eight Fixed Palms»...................17
Chapter 4
Lao Ba Zhang – "Eight Old Palms"...........................33
Chapter 5
 Zhi Tang 64 Zhang - 64 Linear Palms........................52
Chapter 6
Dui Lian – Pair exercises...70
Chapter 7
Bagua Chin-na...103
Chapter 8
Eight main grips...118
 Conclusion...125

Introduction

Dong Haichuan

Baguazhang or "A palm of Eight trigrams – is one of main schools of traditional Chinese Wushu. This style developed in the years of the emperor of Qin dynasty – DaoGuang (1820 – 1850).

The fixed written history of Baguazhang begins from **Dong Haichuan** that is why he is usually named a founder of the school. According to the tradition, he had been born in 1797 in Zhu village, Ju Jia Wu Township, Wen'an County, Hebei Province, and died in1882.

Since his childhood Dong studied martial arts, travelling searching for masters, living in backwoods, till the meeting with a Taoist on Jiu Hua Shan mountain, in An Hui province, who taught him an art of "turning palms, connected with moving round".

In 1862 Dong Haichuan visited Beijing and at the beginning he served in the Prohibited city, then – as a messenger in the residence of the great prince Xu. According to the legend, the prince occasionally had revealed that his servant was an outstanding master of martial arts, so the latter began teaching. Baguazhang spread began in such a way.

Dong Haichuan applied a differentiated approach to pupils, requiring the internal understanding of forms and teaching them, according to natural inclinations and talents. That is why several, very different styles appeared in the course of Baguazhang tradition already in the second generation then they became more numerous.

Let's list main styles and directions of Baguazhang:

Yin Fu style

Yin Fu

Yin Fu master (1840 – 1909) had originated from the capital province, from Ji county and moved to Beijing in youth, there he studied fencing and Lohanquan style. Then he knew that Dong Haichuan had begun teaching and became his pupil.

The direction, founded by Yin master, is characterized by dominating blows, and round steps are used not for coming behind the adversary's spine, but usually for going away from the attack line.

The manner of executing forms is very concentrated, movements are fast, distinct, interrupted. Digs by fingers in pain points and zones on the adversary's body are often used in a combat. A distinctive position of a palm is a "palm – bull tongue", when four fingers are griped and the thumb is pressed to the edge, the whole palm is flat.

At shifting there is often used a "lion step", when a foot rolls from the heel to the tiptoe. The trunk often bends forward.

Cheng Tinghua style

Cheng Tinghua

Among pupils of Dong Haichuan the most famous was **Cheng Tinghua**. He had originated from Shen county, Hebei province and studied hand-to-hand combat and fight since his youth, so his direction contains many goings out behind the adversary's spine and throws. Forms are executed at a high speed, at that movements must be uninterrupted.

A distinctive palm position is a "palm – dragon claws", then fingers a bit bend, the thumb is put forward, the palm center is indrawn, the whole palm is round. At shifting fighters use a step of one "sliding in mud".

Liang Zhenpu style

Liang Zhenpu

Liang Zhenpu (1862 – 1932) was the youngest among Dong Haichuan's pupils, after his teacher's death he continued to improve his mastership, guided be senior pupils. Today the technique of the style includes the forms: "eight fixed palms", "old eight palms", "sixty four palms", "dragon palms" and other.

Gao Yisheng style

Gao Yisheng

Gao Yisheng (1866 – 1951) began to study Baguazhang in 1896, guided by Zhou Yuxiang, who had introduced him to his teacher Cheng Tinghua, who taught Gao till his death in 1900.

Then he continued to study, guided by Zhou till 1911. According to the legend, later he met a Taoist Song Yireng – a pupil of Bi Chengxia) (a teacher of Dong Haichuan). He said Yisheng that, Dong has studied only "Pre-Heaven techniques", but for understanding the system completely, "Post-Heaven techniques" must be also studied. That is why Gao Yisheng's system is divided in two parts "Pre-heaven" and "Post-heaven". The strategy of the system is ciphered in the "Pre-heaven technique" and the tactics – in the "Post-heaven" one. "Pre-heaven" techniques are executed at moving round. "Post-heaven" techniques originate from "Pre-heaven" ones, are divided in eight successions of eight movements, realized at moving straight.

Jiang Rongqiao style

Jiang Rongqiao

Jiang Rongjiao (1891- 1974) was born in Hebei province. Since his childhood he had studied martial arts and perfectly mastered Xingyiquan, Taijiquan Mizhongquan styles. He had taught Baguazhang, guided by Zhang Zhaodong, a pupil of Dong Haichuan, whereupon he created his own style, named "New eight palms", reflected peculiarities of all martial arts, studied by him.

Fu Zhensong

Fu Zhensong

Fu Zhensong (1881 – 1953) was born in Mapo village, Biyang County, Henan province. He was weak and sickly during his childhood. For improving health, he began to practice martial arts. His teachers were: Baguazhang master, Chia Fengming – one of Dong Haichuan's pupils, and Chen Yangxi – Taijiquan master of Chen family.

Having combined the obtained knowledge, Fu Zhengsong created his own direction, a sort of an alloy of Baguazhang andTaijiquan.

Chapter 1
The brief biography of Baguazhang Liang style masters

Liang Zhenpu
(1863 – 1932)

Liang Zhenpu

Liang Zhenpu was born at 12 of May of 1863 in Beihaojia Village in Ji County in Hebei province. His father was an old-cloth dealer and had a store in Beijing, but his mother and two brothers lived in Ji County. He started to study martial arts in the native village Liang. The first style that he mastered was "Springing legs" - **Tantui** that he began to study since seven years old, guided by the famous master Jing Fenyi.

When Liang Zhenpu was fourteen years old, he left his house and moved to Beijing to his father. Having arrived in the capital, he began to study his father's profession, as a result of which his neighbors gave him a nick "Old-cloth dealer Liang".

After one year in Beijing, Liang fell sick. His father often visited the residence of the prince Xu and was acquainted with **Dong Haichuan**. The old Liang asked his master to take his son as a pupil for improving his health and continue to master martial arts. Dong accepted his as a pupil, and difficult days started for Liang Zhenpu.

The new pupil was very diligent in comprehending Baguazhang mysteries. His health improved fast, and he began to progress in martial arts fast.

Liang Zhenpu was the youngest among Dong Haichuan's pupils, so was a favorite of all other master's pupils.

In five years in 1882 after his teacher's death, Liang continued his study, guided by such famous Baguazhang masters as **Yin Fu**, **Cheng Tinghua**, **Zhang Zhaodong**, **Liu Fengchun** and other.

When Liang was twenty years old, his parents died. He had lived for some time at the expanse of selling used things, but then he closed the store and became to earn by teaching martial arts.

When Liang Zhenpu was twenty five years old, he returned to the native village. A band of hooligans was dominating there at this time, but the young master brought it to reason fast.

In 1899, being in the capital, Liang became a witness of an attack of bandits on an artel of carriers of Majiapu station, Beijing – Khankou line. The master intervened in the conflict, and as a result gangsters were dead or traumatized heavily.

Liang Zhenpu was arrested, condemned to death and put in a prison. Due to efforts of Liang's pupil Li Guotai and the master Yin Fu, who worked as a trainer of martial arts in emperor's palace, the convicted person was pardoned, but left in a prison.

At twentieth of July of the same year foreign troops came in Beijing, for finishing the Boxer rebellion. Qin court left the palace. As a result of a battle, a prison house was destructed by a blast that gave a possibility to escape to all prisoners. Liang had returned home, where he lived secretly.

After the finish of the Boxer rebellion that took place near Majiapu, power authorities were not already interested what allowed Liang Zhenpu to left underground and to found a security office.

In 1911after establishing the republic, Liang began to teach Baguazhang in a secondary school of Jixian city. At the instance of Lupingxian sport committee he opened one more school of martial arts. When Liang had created one more security agency, he became a notable person in his county.

At thirteenth of August of 1932 Liang Zhenpu died at the age of sixty nine years, having left a great number of pupils, spread his doctrine throughout China.

Just due to their efforts, Liang Zhenpu Baguazhang direction became the most famous one in Beijing district.

Liang Zhenpu had near twenty close pupils. But the most famous were **Guo Gumin** and **Li Ziming**.

Li Ziming
(1903 – 1993)

Li Ziming

The closest pupil of Liang Zhenpu and his official successor was his fellow-citizen and relative by the female line, Li Ziming.

Li obtained his knowledge in Baguazhang not only from Liang Zhenpu, but also from such famous masters as **Zhang Zhaodong** and **Shang Yuxiang**.

Li Ziming had begun to teach Baguazhang before creation of the Chinese National Republic and continued the business of his whole life even in the years of the "Cultural Revolution". Later he began a founder and permanent head of the "Association for studying Baguazhang", having combined best Baguazhang masters of all styles and directions within it.

Chapter 2
Base principles of Baguazhang

The name **Baguazhang** and its explication originate from the philosophical system, originated from **Yi Jing** (*Book of changes*), written near three thousand years ago. At first having been a manual for fortunetellers, the "Book of changes" had developed in a list of ethic norms, finally became a book of wisdom, one of five classics of Confucianism and a source of Taoist philosophy. The central theme of this work the same way that in the martial system is permanent changes and transformations, laying in the base of whole our existence, and martial art must embody this idea in a system of exercises and defense.

At first the "Book of changes" was a set of linear signs, used for predictions. In one of their meanings these predictions were defined as answers **"yes"** and **"no"**. Thus, "yes" was denoted by a simple continuous line (-) and "no" – by an interrupted one (--).

A necessity to widen notions appeared with time that needed additional lines. Thus, **eight trigrams** (of three lines) appeared at first, then sixty four **hexagrams** (of six lines).

Eight symbols, included in the base of the "Book of changes" are presented below:

Name - Characteristic - Sign - Image
Qian – Creating – Strong - Sky
Kun – Perceiving – Compliant - Land
Zhen – Awakening – Movement - Thunder
Kan – Bottomless – Dangerous - Water
Gen – Keeping calm – Restoring - Mountain
Xun – Soft – Penetrating - Wind
Li – Retentive – Giving light - Fire
Dui – Rejoicing – Enjoying - Lake

In their turn these trigrams form a graph, embodying two orders:

- **Pre-Heaven** succession (internal circle)
- **Post-Heaven** succession (external circle)

On this graph trigram positions are also coordinated with world sides; it is necessary to know that Chinese depict the South above (fig.1).

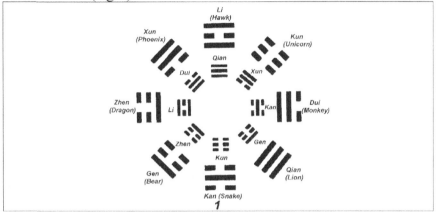

1

The circle of Eight trigrams together with its center form one more important figure, named **"Nine palaces"**. From Ancient times the scheme of Nine palaces served in Taoism as a graphic and numerical model of spiritual improvement, represented by the way to Tao and "return to the world". These two vectors of the Great Way were identified in the Taoist tradition with two types of movement: "Successive" (**Shun**) and "backward" (**Ni**). Nine palaces associated with nine layers of the sky, nine zones of the Land and nine holes of the human body. In old Baguazhang schools they served as an example for training shifts in the space. Thus, for this aim columns of the human height were dug in the ground at the special platform, they played the role of imaginary adversaries.

Pupils moved among these columns in the special order: from the column in the north (**Kan** trigram) – to the South-West (**Kun** trigram), then, having turned this column round, a pupil moved to the East (**Zhen** trigram), then to the North (**Xun** trigram), then by the central column (sometimes running it round) to the North-West (**Qian** trigram), then to the neighboring column in the South-East (**Dui** trigram), to the East again (**Gen** trigram) and finally to the most southern column (**Li** trigram). Then he returns back by the same route (fig.2-4).

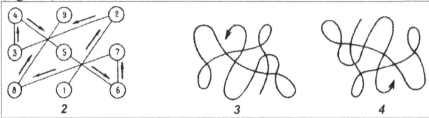

You must not obligatory know nuances of the "book of changes" for practicing hand-to-hand fight, but main notions, presented here, will help to understand the evolution, genesis and principles of the system that are in the permanent movement and flow from one to another that is its force and integrity.

Chapter 3
Ding Shi Ba Zhang – «Eight Fixed Palms"

"Eight Fixed Palms" – is a base form in Baguazhang arsenal.

It is considered, that fixed palms were taught by Dong Haichuan himself, who treated this section of the technique as the most important at school. These exercises create a fundament for practicing round shifts and fixing the upper part of the pelvis in a certain position.

The aim of fixing the upper part of the body is to open muscular-ligamental meridians of the spine and sides for increasing flexibility of the body and to elaborate skills of fast transitions from one position to another.

When a practicing person trains **Ding Shi Ba Zhang**, he must observe three main principles, concerning this section of the technique. The first principle reads that it is necessary to observe the form correctness. The second one – that a Qi energy flow must be unlimited and free. The third principle says that a practicing person must feel how his body fills with force.

At moving round, a practicing person must keep his breath calm, but no instructions, concerning special breath types are given. Thus, the principle of naturalness is realized here.

Each of eight fixed positions has a special physiological and energetic effect on the body.

The relaxed static position of the upper part of the body at moving round and intellectual concentration form the very effective system of health support.

The description of fixed palms:

1. Palms, pressing down

At moving to the right, move your torso to the left. The arms are by sides, the elbows are taken a bit apart, fingers are directed to each other. The look is directed to the circle center. The movement begins from the left leg (fig.1).

Move round from the left leg. Pass one circle, then take the initial position of "Infinite" (legs together, arms are lowered by sides, the spine is straight) or change the direction of your movement by the way, described below.

2. Palms, keeping the sky

At moving to the right, turn your torso to the left, take both palms at first to the breast, then apart. The left leg is taken forward. The look is directed towards the circle center (fig.2).

Move round from the left leg. Pass one circle, then take the initial position of "Infinite" or change the direction of your movement.

3. Palms, embarrassing the moon

At moving to the right, turn your torso to the left. You arms are placed horizontally, the palms are turned to the external side, fingers are pulled to each other, the thumbs are directed down, the elbows are taken apart. The left leg is placed forward. The look is directed towards the circle center (fig.3).

Move round from the left leg. Pass one circle, then take the initial position of "Infinite" or change the direction of your movement.

4. Palms, embarrassing a ball

At moving to the right, turn your torso to the left. The left arm turns palm up and is pulled to the circle center. It remains a bit bent in the elbow, and the elbow is pulled to the ground. The right arm turns palm down and is placed above the head. The left leg is taken forward (fig.4).

Move round from the left leg. Pass one circle, then take the initial position of "Infinite" or change the direction of your movement.

5. Palms, indicating the sky and piercing the ground

At moving to the right, turn your torso to the left. The left arm is pulled up, its palm is turned to you, fingers are pulled up. The right arm is pulled down, the palm is turned to the external side. The left leg is taken forward. The look is directed towards the circle center (fig.5).

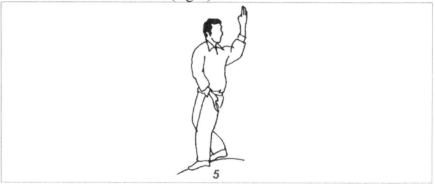

Move round from the left leg. Pass one circle, then take the initial position of "Infinite" or change the direction of your movement.

6. Jin-Yang palms

At moving to the right, turn your torso to the left. The right arm pushes from behind the head forward. The left palm pushes from behind the spine back. The left leg is taken forward (fig.6).

Move round from the left leg. Pass one circle, then take the initial position of "Infinite" or change the direction of your movement.

7. Palms, bearing a pike

At moving to the right, turn your torso to the left. The left arm is pulled horizontally to the circle center, the palm is directed up. The right arm rises above the head, palm up. The left leg is forward. The look is directed to the circle center (fig.7).

Move round from the left leg. Pass one circle, then take the initial position of "Infinite" or change the direction of your movement.

8. Palms, pushing a millstone

At moving to the right, turn your torso to the left. The left palm is directed to the circle center and placed at the face level. The right palm covers the belly. The left leg is taken forward. The look is directed to the circle center (fig.8).

Move round from the left leg. Pass one circle, then take the initial position of "Infinite" or change the direction of your movement by the way, described below.

Form "Eight fixed palms"

Earlier the fixed palms were executed from the initial position – "Infinite" stance then there were added connecting positions, allowing to execute exercises as a continuous succession of movements – a form. In their turn these connecting movements can be complicated or simple.

This book presents the form "Eight fixed palms" with simple connecting exercises.

Initial position – "Infinite" form (fig.1).

1. «Palms, pressing down»

Turn to the right, make the step forward by the left leg. Raise your arms through the sides up, then lower them down, turn your torso to the left and take the left-side position "Palms, pressing down", the look is directed to the circle center (fig.2-5). Move round from the left leg.

Pass one circle, after that change your movement direction. For that, make the step by the right leg, turning your foot inside. Turn to the left. Turn your left foot to the external side. Move your left arm forward and up to the breast level. The left palm is directed to the external side, fingers forward, the thumb is directed down. The right hand is near the belly. Continue to turn to the left, make the step forward by the right leg, turning your foot inside. Both arms are bent in the elbows and placed in front of the breast. Make the piercing movement under the left arm by fingers of the right one, the palm is directed up. The left palm is directed down, fingers are directed to the right (fig.6-9).

Turn your torso to the right and take the right-side position "Palms, pressing down" (fig.10-11).

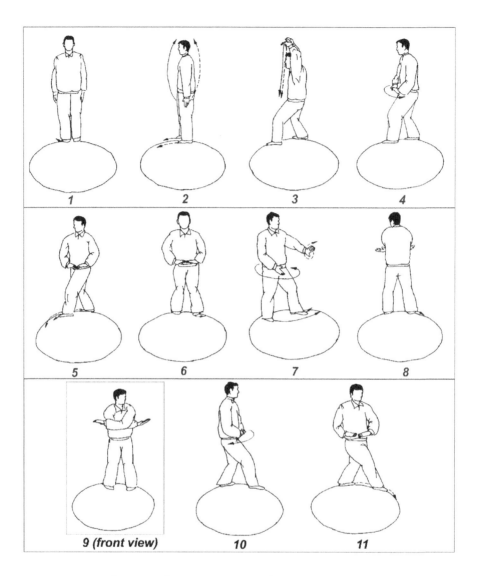

2. «Palms, supporting the sky»

Pass one circle, after that change your movement direction by the aforesaid way and take the left-side position «Palms, supporting the sky» (fig.12-16).

Pass one circle, after that change your movement direction and take the right-side position «Palms, supporting the sky» (fig.17-21).

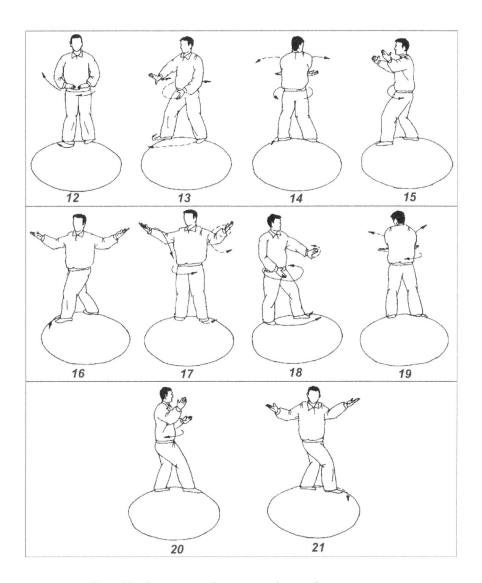

3. «Palms, embarrassing the moon”

Pass one circle, after that change your movement direction and take the left-side position «Palms, embarrassing the Lune” (fig.22-27).

Pass one circle, after that change your movement direction and take the right-side position «Palms, embarrassing the Lune” (fig.28-32).

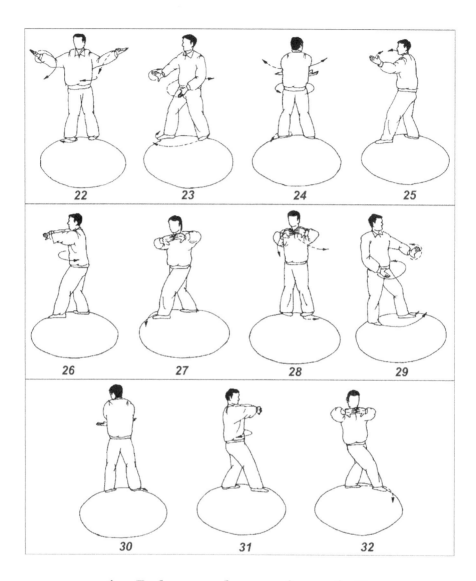

4. «Palms, embarrassing a ball»

Pass one circle, after that change your movement direction and take the left-side position «Palms, embarrassing a ball" (fig.33-37).

Pass one circle, after that change your movement direction and take the right-side position «Palms, embarrassing a ball" (fig.38-41).

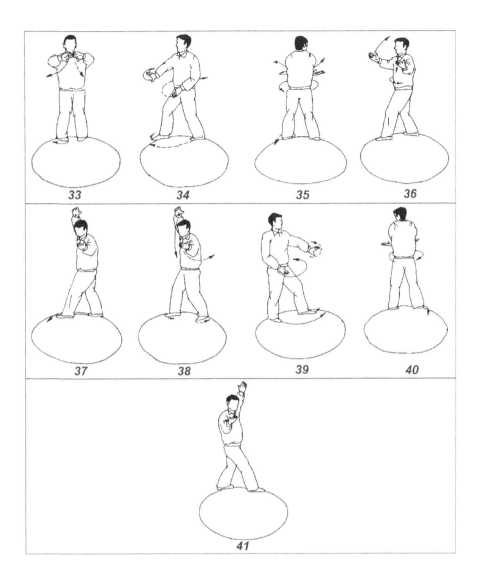

33 34 35 36

37 38 39 40

41

5. «Palms, indicating the sky and piercing the ground»

Pass one circle, after that change your movement direction and take the left-side position «Palms, indicating the sky and piercing the ground» (fig.42-46).

Pass one circle, after that change your movement direction and take the right-side position «Palms, indicating the sky and piercing the ground» (fig.47-51).

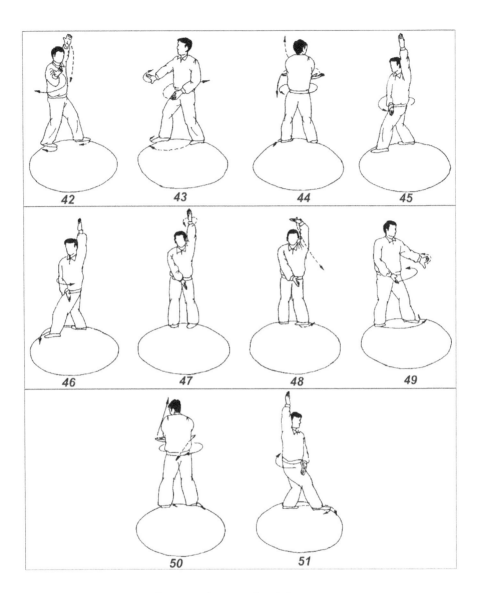

6. «Palms Yin-Yang»

Pass one circle, after that change your movement direction and take the left-side position «Palms Yin-Yang» (fig.52-55).

Pass one circle, after that change your movement direction and take the right-side position «Palms Yin-Yang» (fig.56-59).

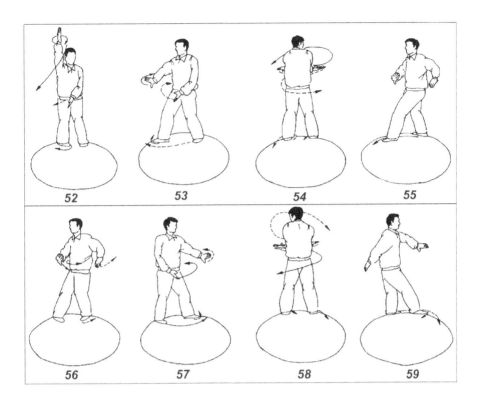

7. «*Palms, bearing a pike*"

Pass one circle, after that change your movement direction and take the left-side position "Palms, bearing a pike" (fig.60-63).

Pass one circle, after that change your movement direction and take the right-side position "Palms, bearing a pike" (fig.64-67).

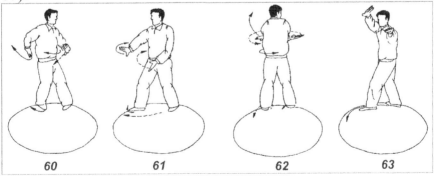

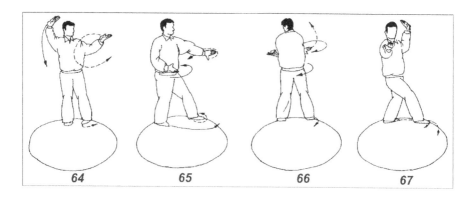

8. «Palms, pushing a millstone»

Pass one circle, after that change your movement direction and take the left-side position «Palms, pushing a millstone» (fig.68-72).

Pass one circle, after that change your movement direction and take the right-side position «Palms, pushing a millstone» (fig.73-77).

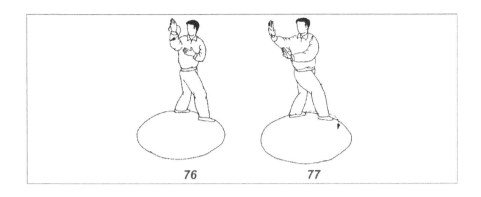

76   77

Final form

Change your movement positions once more and take the initial position (fig.78-86).

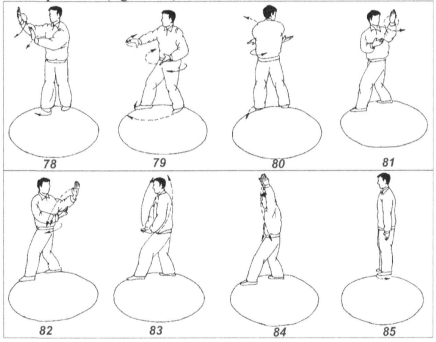

78   79   80   81

82   83   84   85

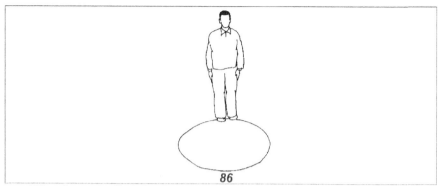

86

The form is finished.

Chapter 4
Lao Ba Zhang – "Eight Old Palms"

After a person, practicing Baguazhang, has mastered the form **"Eight fixed palms"**, he begins to study the form **"Eight Old Palms"**. If in **Ding Shi Ba Zhang** the main aim is the method of going and qigong, and changes are secondary, in **Lao Ba Zhang** changes become primary, because a practicing person feels himself confidently in stances and movement now.

Despite the fact that this form also favors **Qi** development, the initial aim is to focus attention on shifts. At training **"Eight Old Palms"** there is studied how changes must be executed, how to get a clear understanding about the martial application of studied techniques, how to throw efforts — **Jing** at their execution. It is necessary to understand and feel, how models of throwing efforts change, depending on transferring from one form to another. It allows to vary the technique and to use Jing spontaneously in any situation, created in a certain moment of a combat.

At training "Eight Old Palms" it is necessary to observe eight main principles: a correct form, an unlimited Qi flow, fullness with energy, smoothness of changes, understanding of martial application, understanding of Jing use, understanding of a theory or method.

Observance of these principles demonstrates the pupil's readiness to understand, how eight directions (four direct and four angled) are involved in own expression of Yin and Yang.

There are eight base methods of using each of "eight direct" and "eight angled".

Having taken eight directions and having connected them with each of eight methods, we can get sixty four methods of expressing or changing this technique. The eighth principle is the understanding of martial changes that is the study of how an adversary can change as a response to your technique, and how you can apply your technique for counteracting maneuvers, used by an opponent for a counterattack, effectively.

The form description

The initial position

Make the step by the right leg along the circle line from the "Infinite" stance. Turn your torso to the right, the arms move to the right. The right palm is directed to the external side, the left one is directed up and placed under the right arm. Make the step by the left leg forward and turn the torso to the left. The arms take the position "Palms, pushing a millstone" and are directed to the circle center (1-4).

Single Changing Palm
(Dan Huan Zhang)

The initial position – is the left-side stance "Palms, pushing a millstone".

Begin to move along the circle to the right from the left leg. After passing one circle, make the step by the right leg and lower it in front of the left one, having turned the foot inside strongly.

The left am is taken to the right shoulder, the right one is placed near the low part of the belly. The torso is turned by 90 degrees to the left. Continuing the movement, turn by 90 degrees to the left once more, in such a way changing your movement direction. The left arm is taken forward, its palm is directed up, fingers – forward. Make the step forward by the right leg. Synchronously with it strike the direct piercing blow by fingers of the right hand forward at the throat level. The palm of the striking arm is directed to the left. Immediately after the blow, turn your torso to the right. The arms take the position "Palms, pushing a millstone" and are directed to the circle center (fig.5 – 9).

Pass one circle to the left from the right leg then make the form "Palm of a single change" to the other side.

Covering Palm
(Gai Zhang)

Move round to the right from the left leg from the initial position. Having passed approximately one circle, make the step forward by the left leg. Synchronously with it, make the block from outside inside by the left forearm at the face level. The right arm defends the belly. Make the step forward by the right leg. Synchronously with it, make the block, analogous to the previous one by the right arm. The left arm moves on arc down, back and up behind the head.

Strike the direct kick forward by the left leg at the middle or upper level. Take the left palm from behind the head forward and make the clap on the left instep by it. Lower the left leg down and back, turn to the left by 180 degrees and strike the blows by both palm ribs in the sides at the low level.

Transfer the most part of the body weight on the lead left leg and take the left-side lunge stance – Gong Bu. Raise the left arm up-forward palm forward. Make the step by the right leg.

Synchronously with the step, strike the piercing blow by fingers of the right hand. Turn by 180 degrees to the left and turn the left foot to the external side. Make the step forward by the right leg.

Synchronously with it move the right arm round back-up, then take it from behind the head and strike the blow by the palm forward-down.

Turn to the left by 180 degrees and turn the left foot to the turn side. Synchronously with it strike the double blow by the palm ribs on the sides at the low level.

Transfer the most part of the body weight on the lead left leg and take the left-side lunge position – Gong Bu. Raise the left arm forward – up to the horizontal level.

Make the step forward by the right leg. Synchronously with it strike the direct piercing blow by fingers of the right hand forward at the throat level.

Turn the torso to the right. The palms take the position "Palms, pushing a millstone" and are directed to the circle center (fig. 10 – 23).

Pass round to the left from the right leg then make the form "Covering palm" to the other side.

Turning Back Palm
(Fan Bei Zhang)

Pass round to the right from the left leg from the initial position. After making the step by the left leg, turn to the right by 180 degrees and make the step by the left leg to the right one. Both toes are directed to each other. Both arms are crossed near the breast in such a way that the right one is under the left one.

Then turn by 180 degrees to the right and raise the right leg, bent in the knee. Lower the right leg down-forward, then make the step forward by the left leg. Synchronously with it strike the blow by the palms, put together, at the belly level.

Turn to the right, then turn the right foot maximally to the right, continue to turn to the right and make the step by the left leg to the turn side. Make the little step to the right by the right leg and take the high Ma Bu stance, the look is directed to the circle center. Strike the blow up by the palms, put together.

Turn by 360 degrees to the right. For that at first make the step towards the turn by the left leg then make the step by the right leg in your movement direction. You are in Ma Bu stance again, your face to the circle center. Synchronously with it strike the double blow by both palm ribs to the sides at the low level.

Transfer the body weight on the left leg. Take the right leg to the left one and lower it on the toe. Make the block from outside inside at the upper level by the right arm. The left arm is near the left side. Make the step to the right by the right leg and transfer the body weight on it. Take the left leg to the right one and lower it on the toe. Make the block from outside inside by the left arm at the upper level. The right arm is near the right side.

Make the step to the left by the left leg and take the left-side lunge stance – Gun Bu. Strike the chopping blow top-down and forward by left palm rib. Make the step forward by the right leg and strike the direct piercing blow by fingers of the right hand forward.

Turn the torso to the right. The arms take the position "Palms, pushing a millstone" and are directed to the circle center (fig.24 – 39).

Pass round to the left from the right leg, then make the form "Palm, turning back" to the other side.

Chopping Palm
(Pi Zhang)

Pass round to the right from the left leg from the initial position. Make the step forward by the right leg and lower it in front of the left one, turning the foot inside strongly. The left arm is taken to the right shoulder. The right arm defends the belly.

Turn to the left and make the step by the left leg to the opposite direction. Take the left arm forward. Its palm is directed up. Make the step forward by the right leg and strike the piercing blow by fingers of the right hand forward.

Turn the right foot to the left then turn the left foot too. After that, turn the torso in the same direction. The right hand is taken to the left shoulder, its palm is directed back. The left arm is pressed to the belly, the palm is directed down. Continuing to turn to the left, make the step by the left leg in the movement direction. Strike the chopping blow top-down and forward by the left palm rib. Make the step forward by the right leg and strike the direct piercing blow by fingers of the right hand forward.

Turn to the left, make the step by the left leg to the turn direction and strike the chopping blow by the left palm rib top-down and forward. Make the step forward by the right leg and strike the direct piercing blow by fingers of the right hand forward.

Turn to the left and make the step by the left leg to the turn direction. Synchronously with it strike the chopping blow by the left palm rib top-down and forward.

Make the step forward by the right leg. Synchronously with the step, strike the piercing blow by fingers of the right hand forward. Turn the torso to the right. The arms take the position "Palms, pushing a millstone" and are directed to the circle center (fig.40 – 53).

Pass round to the left from the right leg then make the form "Chopping palm" to the other side.

Following Trough Palm
(Shun Shi Zhang)

Pass round to the right from the left leg from the initial position. Make the step forward by the right leg and lower it in front of the left one, turning the foot inside strongly. Turn to the left and make the step by the left leg in the opposite direction. The left arm is taken forward, its palm is directed up.

Make the step forward by the right leg and turn by 180 degrees to the left. The right arm moves up from under the left one. Bend the leg in the knee and raise it up.

Lower the right leg down-to the right and take the right-side stance Pu Bu. The left arm is pulled along the left leg, its palm is directed to the left. The right arm remains pulled up, its palm is directed up. Transfer the most part of the body weight on the lead left leg and take the left-side lunge position – Gong Bu. Make the piercing movement by fingers of the left hand forward, the palm is directed up. The right arm is pulled back – down and twisted in such a way that its palm is directed up.

Turn to the right, take the right-side lunge stance– Gong Bu and make the movement, analogous to the previous one. Turn to the left, take the left-side stance Gong Bu and make the analogous movement once more. Make the step forward by the right leg. Synchronously with it, strike the direct piercing blow by fingers of the right hand forward.

Turn the torso to the right. The arms take the position "Palms, pushing a millstone" and are directed to the circle center (fig. 54 – 64).

Pass round to the left from the right leg then make the form "Following palm" to the other side.

Following Step Palm
(Shun Bu Zhang)

Pass round to the right from the left leg from the initial position. Make the step forward by the right leg and lower it in front of the left one, turning the foot inside strongly. Turn to the left and make the step by the left leg in the opposite direction. The left arm is taken forward, its palm is directed up.

Make the step forward by the right leg. Synchronously with it, strike the piercing blow by fingers of the right hand forward. At the blow the torso turns to the left. At first turn the right foot inside, then turn the left one outside. The torso continues to turn to the left. Both arms are taken to the right and up.

Make the step back by the left leg. Both hands are squeezed in the fists and taken down to the right shin.

Turn by 180 degrees to the left and make the step forward by the right leg. Both arms move on arc up-forward, then take the position "Palms, pushing a millstone" and are directed to the circle center (fig. 65 – 71).

Pass round to the left from the right leg then make the form "Palm of the Following step" to the other side.

Pushing Down Palm
(Xia Ta Zhang)

Pass round to the right from the left leg from the initial position. After passing one circle, make the step by the right leg and lower it in front of the left one, turning the foot inside strongly. The left arm is taken to the right shoulder, the right one is near the low part of the belly. The torso turns by 90 degrees to the left. Continuing the movement, turn by 90 degrees to the left once more and make the step by the left leg, in such a way changing the movement position. The left arm is taken forward, its palm is directed up, fingers – forward. Make the step forward by the right leg. At that strike the direct piercing blow by fingers of the right hand forward at the throat level. The striking palm is directed to the left.

Turn by 180 degrees to the left. Make the step forward by the right leg. Synchronously with it strike the blow from behind the head forward by the right palm, and make the piercing movement back at the low level by fingers of the left hand.

Turn by 180 to the left. The left palm is taken to the belly and directed down. Continue to turn to the left. The left arm moves up, the right one is taken forward.

Make the step forward by the right leg. Synchronously with it, strike the piercing blow by fingers of the right hand forward at the belly level, its palm is directed up.

Turn to the left and continue the aforesaid movement twice more. After that continue to rotate to the left and make the step back-to the right by the right leg. You are in the position with your face, directed to the circle center. Synchronously with it strike the double blow by the back sides of the hands to the sides.

Transfer the body weight on the right leg and pull the left one to the right one. The right leg touches the floor surface only by the toe. The left arm makes the block from outside inside at the upper level. The right palm is placed near the right side.

Make the step forward by the left leg. Synchronously with the step strike the chopping blow by the left palm rib top-down and forward.

Make the step forward by the right leg. Synchronously with it strike the direct piercing blow by fingers of the right hand forward.

Turn the torso to the left. The arms take the position "Palms, pushing a millstone" and are directed to the circle center (fig. 72 – 94).

Pass round to the left from the right leg then make the form "Palm pushing down" to the other side.

Flat Piercing Palm
(Pin Chuan Zhang)

Pass round to the right from the left leg from the initial position. Make the step forward by the right leg and lower it in front of the left one. The left arm is taken to the right shoulder. The right arm defends the belly. Make the step forward by the left leg to the opposite direction. Take the left arm forward, its palm is directed up, fingers are directed forward.

Make the step forward by the right leg. Synchronously with it strike the direct piercing blow by fingers of the right hand forward. The right palm is directed down.

After that, make two more steps, synchronously striking two successive piercing blows by fingers of the left and right hands forward.

Turn to the left. Turn the left foot to the external side. Make the step by the right leg forward. Synchronously with it strike the blow by the right palm from behind the head forward. The left arm pierces back-down.

Continue to turn to the left. Make the step back by the left leg and take the left-side stance Pu Bu. The left arm is pulled along the left leg, its palm is directed to the left. The right arm is pulled back-up, its palm is directed up.

Transfer the most part of the body weight on the lead left leg and take the left-side lunge stance – Gong Bu. The left arm is raised forward-up to the horizontal position.

Make the step forward by the right leg. Synchronously with it strike the direct piercing blow by fingers of the right hand forward, its palm is directed to the left. Turn the torso to the right. The arms take the position "Palms, pushing a millstone" and are directed to the circle center (fig. 95 – 105).

Pass round to the left from the right leg, then make the form "Flat piercing palm" to the other side.

Final position

When you have executed the last exercise of the form "Eight old palms", you are in the left-side stance with "Palms, pushing a millstone".

Pass a circle to the right, after that make the step forward by the right leg, turning the foot inside. The left arm moves to the right shoulder, the right arm defends the belly.

Make the step back-to the left by the left leg, having turned your face to the circle center and take the stance Ma Bu. Strike the chopping blows to the sides at the low level by both palm ribs.

Put the right leg near the left one. Raise both arms through the sides up. Unbend the legs in the knees, straighten yourself and lower your arms down (fig.106 – 109).

Chapter 5
Zhi Tang 64 Zhang - 64 Linear Palms

The form **"Sixty four palms"** is one of basic in Baguazhang arsenal.

It consists of eight forms, each of them in its turn consists of eight techniques, executed by the straight line. Thus, practicing persons train sixty four maneuvers that may be used in a combat together with methods of round movement and changes.

The main idea of the form is that each movement, made by Baguazhang fighter, can be opposed only by a limited number of adversary's ones. Each following technique in this form corresponds to the most probable counterattack that may be expected from an opponent as a response to a previous movement.

The form consists of blows by arms, kicks by legs, throws and pain maneuvers.

The form description

The Initial position

The initial position for each of eight Lu – «tracks» of Zhi Tang 64 Zhang form is a right-side stance "A monk holds a cup". The right leg is put forward, and near twenty five percents of the body weight are on it. The most part of the body weight is on the rear left leg. The hips are relaxed, the pelvis is lowered, the spine is arched, he breast is concaved and empty, the shoulders are lowered, the neck is straightened.

The right arm is bent in the elbow and directed up, the elbow is pulled down, the palm is directed up, the finger tips are at the nose level.

The left arm is placed horizontally near the belly, its palm is directed forward-down. The look is directed straight. This stance is taken, making the step back by the left leg (fig.1–2).

The first track
(Yi Lu)

Make the step forward by the left leg and substep by the right leg from the initial position of the right-side stance "A monk holds a cup". The left arm moves up, its palm is directed to the right, the thumb is directed up. Strike the direct blow by the right palm forward at the breast level.

Both hands form fists and are taken to the breast. Make the chasse step forward by the right leg. Both arms are taken forward, striking piercing blows forward. The right arm turns palm up and pierces at the belly level. The left arm turns palm down and pierces at the level a bit upper the head.

The left palm is laid on the right forearm near the wrist. The right arm makes the rotating movement around its axis then is abruptly taken forward, striking the blow by the back side of the hand. Synchronously with it, make the chasse step forward by the right leg.

Make the step forward by the left leg, then make the substep forward by the right leg. Make the covering movement by the left palm at the breast level. Strike the side punch by the right fist at the head level.

Make the chasse step forward by the left leg. Make the block from inside outside by the left forearm at the upper level, the hand is squeezed in the fist. Synchronously with it, strike the direct punch forward at the belly level.

Make one more chasse step by the left leg forward. Make the covering movement by the left palm. Synchronously with it strike the chopping punch by the back side of the right fist.

Make the big step back by the right leg and transfer the most part of the body weight on the right leg, bent in the knee. The left leg is straightened in the knee. Turn the torso to the right. The right hand is squeezed in the fist and taken to the right side. The left arm is pulled and pushes forward-down with an effort, its palm is directed down.

Catch the right forearm near the wrist by the left hand. Make the step forward by the right leg. Turn by 180 degrees to the left, turning the left foot to the external side. The right elbow is directed forward.

Make the step back by the left leg and take the right-side stance "A monk holds a cup" (fig.3–11).

The second track
(Er Lu)

Make the step forward by the left leg, after that substep by the right leg. Make the covering movement by the left palm. The right palm moves on arc and strikes the blow from behind the head forward.

Make the chasse step by the left leg. Make the covering movement by the left palm. Strike the direct punch by the right fist forward at the belly level.

Make one more chasse step by the left leg. Make the covering movement by the left palm. Strike the piercing blow forward at the head level by fingers of the right hand.

Make the little step forward by the right leg, after that make the big step by the left leg. Strike the piercing blow forward at the head level by fingers of the left hand. The left palm is directed up. The right hand is taken to the right side.

Make the step forward by the right leg. Strike the round blow by the right elbow at the middle level. The left palm covers the right forearm.

Make the step to the left by the right leg, beginning to turn to the left by 360 degrees. At the end of the turn make the step by the left leg in the turn direction. Strike the blow by the left elbow from yourself at the middle level. The right palm is laid on the left fist, intensifying the attack.

Make the chasse step forward by the left leg. Make the covering movement by the left palm. Strike the side punch at the head level by the right fist.

Make the chasse step forward by the left leg. Both hands turn palms forward, fingers are directed towards each other. Strike the direct blow forward from yourself by both palms. At the end of the movement hands are taken a bit aside, as if breaking something.

Turn by 180 degrees to the right and take the right-side stance "A monk holds a cup" (fig.12–21).

56

The third track
(San Lu)

Make the little step forward by the right leg from the initial position. Both arms move on arcs to the external sides then they are joined by the palm bases near the belly. Make the step forward by the left leg then substep by the right leg. Strike the blow-push forward by both palms at the belly level. Fingers of both hands are directed to the external sides.

Make the step forward by the right leg then substep by the left leg. Both palms don't change their position. Strike one more blow by them – push forward bottom-up at the head level.

Turn the right foot inside, then turn by 180 degrees to the left and take Ma Bu stance. Immediately after the turn, strike the short blow by both elbows in the sides.

Make the chasse step forward by the left leg. Synchronously with it, strike the coupled blow forward by both palms. Fingers are directed towards each other.

Make the big step forward by the left leg. The right arm is taken to the torso, its palm is directed down. Strike the direct blow forward by the left palm; fingers of the attacking extremity are directed to the right.

Take the left leg back and lower it on the ground on the toe. The left arm turns palm up and rises a bit up. The right arm rises up above the head.

Step behind the left leg by the right one and take the crossed position. The left forearm rises up above the head, the palm is directed up. Strike the direct blow at the breast level by the right palm.

Make the step back by the right leg. Both hands are squeezed in the fists and taken to the left knee.

Make the step forward by the left leg. Two arms are taken forward, the palms are directed up, the right palm is near the left elbow bend.

Turn by 180 degrees to the right and take the right-side stance "A monk holds a cup" (fig.22 – 31).

The fourth track
(Si Lu)

Put the right leg to the left one, abruptly twisting the body to the left. The right arm is taken to the right and back, its fingers are pulled to the ground, the left arm covers the breast, its palm is directed outside.

The right arm rises fast, moving on arc up and to the right, the torso also twists to the right. Then the right arm moves to the breast. You imitate the block from inside outside, the grip of the adversary's extremity and its lead to the right and down.

Strike the direct blow forward by fingers of the left hand, its palm is directed down.

The right leg makes the little step to the right, abruptly stamping the foot. Make the step forward and to the left by the left leg, putting the foot at the same level with the right one. You are in the frontal Ma Bu stance. Strike the double side fist by both fists at the breast level.

Rotate to the left by 270 degrees on the left leg, at the end of the movement make the step by the right leg to the rotation side. Strike chopping punches to by the back sides of both fists the sides.

The right arm is taken down by the abrupt movement, its palm is placed near the right hip, the hand is squeezed in the fist. The left arm bends in the elbow, its palm is taken to the right shoulder and turned outside. Make the chasse step forward by the left leg. Strike the blow at the low level by the straightened right arm. It is stricken y the back side of the fist.

Make the step forward by the right leg. The torso turns to the right. Both palms are taken apart, they are directed to the external sides.

Make the step back by the left leg. The left hand is squeezed in the fist and taken to the right side. The right palm presses forward and down.

Turn to the right and make the step forward by the right leg. Both hands are squeezed in the fists. The right fist is taken to the right from the head, the arm is bent in the elbow. The left elbow presses up.

Make the chasse step forward by the left leg. The left palm is taken down-to the left to the homonymous side. Strike the ascending fist forward-up at the head level by the right fist.

Make the step forward by the right leg, turning its foot inside. Turn by 180 degrees to the left and take the right-side stance "A monk holds a cup" (fig.32–41).

The fifth track
(Wu Lu)

Turn approximately by 90 degrees to the left from the initial position. The arms are crossed near the breast, the left arm is above the right one. Continuing to turn to the left, raise the left leg, bent in the knee. Make the piercing movement up from under the left arm by fingers of the right one. The left palm defends the torso.

Lower the left leg forward-down. Strike the blow from yourself at the low level by the left palm rib.

Strike the round blow in the horizontal plane from the right to the left by the right palm rib. The left palm moves towards the right elbow bend. Synchronously with it, strike the direct kick at the knee level by the right leg.

Lower the right leg down. It must be put besides the left leg, stamping the foot not strongly. Strike the punch forward and top-down by the right fist; fingers are directed to the external side. The left palm defends the belly. The look is directed forward.

The right leg steps back, the right fist is unclenched, the right arm moves forward and up, then lowers down, its palm is directed up. After substepping by the left leg, strike the low direct kick forward on the shin of the imaginary adversary by the right toe.

Lower the right leg down and back. Move the left arm on arc from the belly to the left, making the sweeping movement to the external side. Immediately after that, strike the side punch by the right fist at the head level.

Make the step forward by the left leg. Take the right arm to the homonymous side. Synchronously with it, strike the direct blow forward at the head level by fingers of the left hand.

Make the chasse step forward by the right leg. Strike the direct piercing blow forward by fingers of the right hand, its palm is directed to the left.

Make the chasse step forward by the right leg. Catch the right forearm by the left hand, after that turn by 180 degrees to the left. The right elbow is directed forward.

Make the step back by the left leg and take the right-side stance "A monk holds a cup" (fig.42–52).

The sixth track
(Liu Lu)

Make the step back from the initial position by the right leg and pull the left leg to it, the left foot is on the toe. Bend both knees and "lower" down. Clench both hands in the fists and take them to the left knee. Make the big step forward by the left leg. Synchronously strike the blow-push by the closed palms forward. Fingers of the right hand are directed up, fingers of the left one are directed down. This hands position is often known as "Palms – butterflies".

Make the step forward-to the right by the right leg. Take your arms apart.

Make the step by the left leg forward. Make the covering movement by the right palm then strike the ascending punch by the left fist forward-up.

Make the step back by the left leg. Immediately after that, strike the kick by the right knee up. Both arms move to the right.

Make the chasse step forward by the right leg. Synchronously with it, strike the ascending punch forward-up.

Make the chasse step forward by the right leg. Make the covering movement by the left palm. The right hand takes the "hook" form and is taken up, moving on arc. Make the step forward by the left leg then substep by the right leg in the same direction. Make the block up by the left arm. Synchronously with it, strike the direct blow by the right palm forward.

Turn by 180 degrees to the right and take the right-side stance "A monk holds a cup" fig.53–61).

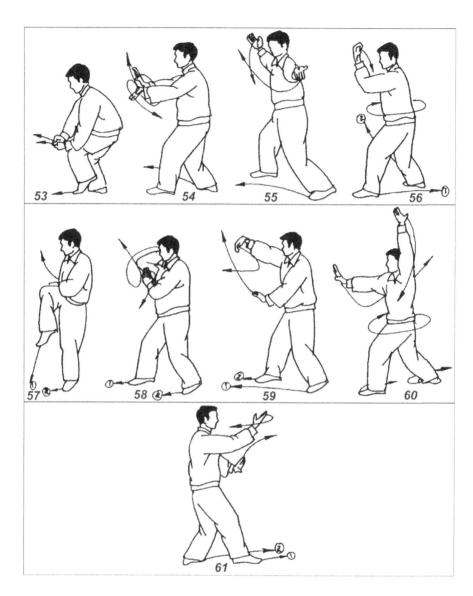

Seventh track
(Qi Lu)

Make the step forward by the right leg from the initial position. Clench the right hand in the fist and take it back behind the right ear. Make the step forward by the left leg. Clench the left hand in the fist and strike the direct punch at the upper level.

Make the chasse step forward by the left leg. Strike the direct punch by the right fist forward at the head level; fingers of the striking extremity are directed outside. The left fist is taken to the breast.

Unclench the right fist and take it back to the breast. Make the little step back by the left leg. Strike the kick forward and top-down at the knee level by the right heel; the toe of the striking extremity turns outside.

Lower the right leg on the ground. After that, make the chasse step forward by the left leg. Strike the direct blow – push forward by both palms. Fingers of both hands are directed to each other, the thumbs are directed down.

The left arm is taken to the breast. The right one imitates the grip of the adversary's extremity, after which he makes the jerk back. Strike the swinging kick forward-up by the right leg, the heel is taken forward, toes are pulled back.

Lower the right leg on the ground, make the step forward by the left leg, after that turn by 360 degrees to the right and strike the punch by the back side of the right fist in the horizontal plane from inside outside at the middle level. The left palm is near the right elbow bend.

Make the little step back by the left leg, after that pull the right leg back too. The left palm makes the covering movement top-down. The right arm is taken back, then abruptly moves forward and up, its hand is squeezed in the fist.

Make the big step forward by the left leg. The right arm is abruptly taken up, twisted around its axis inside, its palm is straightened and directed down. The left arm is also pulled forward at the middle level, its palm is directed up.

Turn by 180 degrees to the right and take the right-side stance "A monk holds a cup" (fig.62–70).

The eighth track
(Ba Lu)

Make the step forward by the left leg from the initial position, at that turning the foot inside and the torso a bit to the right. Strike the direct piercing blow forward by fingers of the left hand. The right palm is taken to the left elbow bend.

Make the step forward by the right leg and strike the analogous piercing blow by fingers of the right hand.

Make the chasse step back by the left leg and take the right-side stance Xu Bu. Both arms are taken to the breast then they strike the coupled blow by the palms top-down. The palm bases are joined, fingers are directed to the sides.

Make the chasse step forward by the right leg. The arms are abruptly raised up to the chin level, the palms are turned up, fingers are pulled forward.

Make the little step forward by the right leg, stamping the foot slightly. Make the covering movement by the left palm. Make the big step forward by the right leg, turning the foot to the left strongly. Bend your torso to the left.

Strike the side blow at the upper level by the right arm. It is stricken by the back side of the right hand, the arm is almost straightened in the elbow.

Make another big step forward by the left leg, the foot is turned outside. Strike the kick bottom-up and outside-inside by the left knee. Make the cutting movement from the left to the right by the left palm rib, the elbow is pressed to the torso.

Strike the side blow by the right palm at the face level, the elbow bends at that.

Lower the right leg down and to the left, taking the crossed stance. Both arms are taken apart, the palms are directed down.

Turn by 180 degrees to the left then make the step forward by the right leg. Synchronously with it, strike the chopping blow by the right palm rib bottom-up on the left palm.

Make the big step forward by the right leg and take Ban Ma Bu stance. Raise the left forearm above the head. Synchronously with it, strike the direct blow forward by the left palm.

Turn by 180 degrees to the left and take the right-side stance "A monk holds a cup" (fig.71–80).

The final position

Put the right leg to the left one. Straighten your knees. Straighten the torso and lower both arms down (fig.81).

The form is finished

Chapter 6
Dui Lian – Pair exercises

After studying the form "Sixty eight palms", practicing persons begin to train skills of application of the studied techniques. One of most important elements of this section is pair forms – **Dui Lian**.

The pair form, offered to your attention, is completely constructed, based on the single form **Zhi Tang 64 Zhang**, studied earlier, and is adapted for training Baguazhang martial techniques by **two partners**.

The initial position

You and your partner are in front of each other. Make the steps towards each other by the right legs and cross your right arms. The left ones defend the torsos (fig.1-2).

The first track
(Yi Lu)

Take the adversary's right arm up by the left palm. Make the step forward by the left leg. Synchronously with the step, strike the direct blow by the right palm in the breast (fig.3,4).

The adversary makes the step back by the left leg. He knocks your attacking arm down by the left palm and catches it.

Make the step forward by the right leg. Catch the adversary's right arm by the left hand and pull it down. Synchronously with it, move your right arm up, crossing the adversary's arms in such a way. It is easy to release your right arm from the grip in this position, snatching it out towards the opponent's left thumb.

Control the adversary's right arm by the left palm, and take your right arm at first to the belly then strike the piercing blow by fingers in the groin or belly (fig.5,6).

The adversary makes the step back by the right leg and knocks your blow down again by the left palm.

Catch the opponent's left hand by your left one, twist it palm rib up, and then lay your right hand on it. This action causes the acute pain in the hand and forces the adversary to bend forward.

Using this moment, make the little substep by the right leg forward and take the right arm forward to the adversary's breast by the rubbing movement, without stopping to press down by the hand. This movement must force the adversary to lower down on the knees because of the acute pain (fig.7,8).

A single moment for the opponent to defend himself from this attack is to put his right arm under your right one that doesn't give a possibility to continue pressing his wrist.

For continuing your attack, knock his right arm down by your left one. Make the step forward by the left leg and strike the side punch in the head by the right fist (fig.9,10).

The adversary makes the step back by the right leg and throws his left arm forward-up, in such a way blocking your punch.

Make the chasse step forward by the left leg, make the blocking movement from inside outside by the left forearm, fixing the opponent's arm in the high position. Strike the direct punch by the right fist in the open left part of the adversary's torso (fig.11,12).

The adversary makes one more step back and knocks your punch down by the right palm.

Knock his right arm down by the left palm. Make the chasse step forward by the left leg. Synchronously with it, strike the chopping punch by the back side of the right fist in the face (fig.13).

The adversary knocks your left arm down by his left one, he has time to put his right arm under the punch.

Catch his right wrist by the right arm and put your left palm on his elbow. Make the step back by the right leg and make the lever of the elbow, pressing down and forcing the adversary to bend (fig.14).

Before you have finished the martial maneuver, the adversary knocks your grip down by the left arm.

Catch the adversary's arm by the left hand at first then by the right one. Turn your right shoulder to him. After that, pull the caught arm forward and up, put your right hip to his torso and make a throw (fig.15-17).

For defending himself, the adversary leans his right palm on your right shoulder and step over your right leg by his right one.

You and your opponent turn, take the right-side stances and cross your right arms.

Now you can make all exercises of this form, having changed places with the opponent.

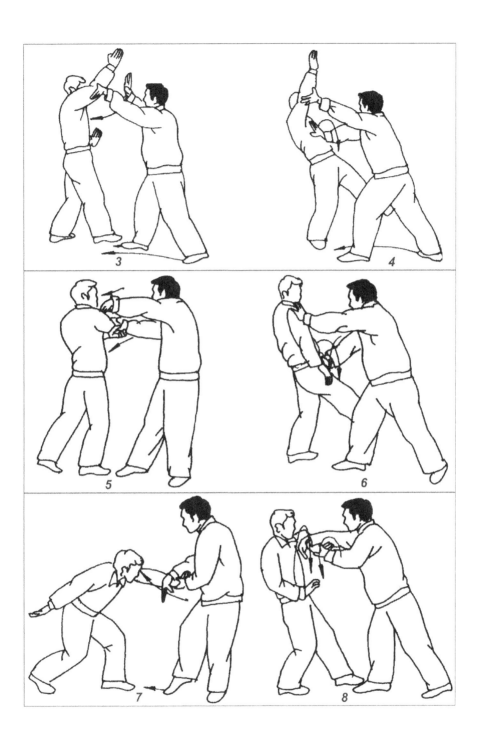

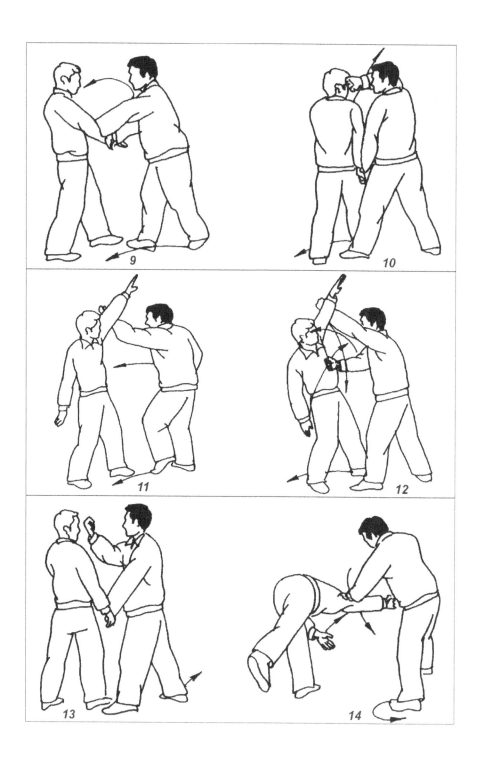

15

16

17

The second track
(Er Lu)

Knock the adversary's right arm down by the left one from the initial position. Make the step forward by the left leg. Synchronously with the step, strike the blow by the right palm in the adversary's neck or shoulder (fig.18, 19).

The adversary makes the step back by the right leg and knocks your attacking arm down by his left one. Make the half-step back by the right leg. Knock his left arm down by your left one, after that, make the chasse step forward by the left leg with synchronous punch in the belly by the right fist (fig.20, 21).

The adversary blocks your attacking arm by his right one. Take his arm away by your left one, make the chasse step forward by the left leg, unclenching the right fist in the palm, and strike the abrupt direct piercing blow in the eyes (fig.22).

The adversary defends himself from your blow by the left arm. Make the big step forward by the left leg and step behind the opponent's lead leg. Take his left arm to the external side by the right arm. The torso abruptly turns to the right. Synchronously with it, make the sweeping movement by the left arm from the right to the left, having placed the attacking extremity under the opponent's left arm (fig.23).

The adversary blocks your attack by his right arm. Continuing to twist to the left, make the step forward by the right leg and strike the round blow by the right elbow in the adversary's breast (fig.24).

The adversary tries to defend himself from your attack by the right arm and to escape to the left. Turn by 180 degrees to the left and strike the blow by the left elbow in the breast or solar plexus (fig.25, 26).

The adversary knocks your elbow down. As a response your catch his right arm by your left hand and take it down. Make the chasse step forward by the left leg and strike the side punch by the right fist in the head (fig.27, 28).

The adversary tries to knock your attacking arm down by his left one. As a response you take your palms together in the center, make the step forward by the left leg and break the adversary's defense, taking his arms apart and getting a possibility to attack his neck and shoulder zone (fig.29, 30).

The adversary can circle your arms by his right arm and pulls it forward and up, blocking your attack.

In the final phase of movements you and your opponent are in the initial position with the crossed right arms.

Now you can make all exercises of this form, having changed places with the opponent.

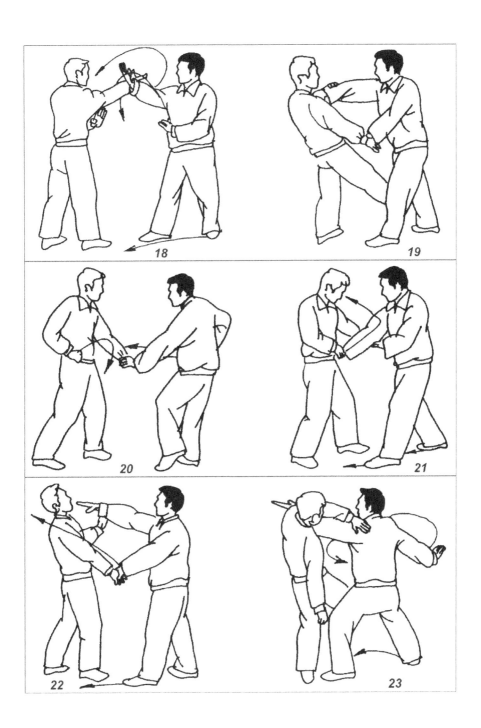

24

25

26
front view

27

28

29

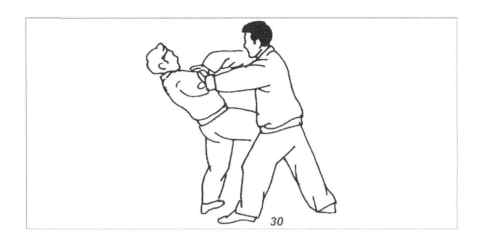

The third track
(San Lu)

Pull your left arm forward from under the right one, in such a way opening the adversary's defense. Rotate the joint palms counterclockwise, opening the opponent for your attack, after that synchronously with the big step forward by the left leg, make the strong push by two arms in the center of the adversary's breast (fig.31, 32).

The adversary puts his shoulders together, preventing your attack. Make the step forward by the right leg and strike the coupled blow by both palms bottom-up in the adversary's chin (fig.33, 34).

The adversary moves both arms bottom-up and raises your attacking extremities. Turn by 180 degrees to the left and strike the blow by the left elbow in the solar plexus with the turn (fig.35).

The adversary blocks this attack by the right palm. Turn the torso to the left, circle his right arm by your left one, and his left one – by your right one. After that, attack his face by both palms, making the step forward by the left leg (fig.36, 37).

The adversary has caught your left arm by his right hand. Catch his left arm by the right hand and pull it on yourself. Synchronously with it, attack his eyes by your left palm, sending a movement impulse from the spine (fig.38, 39).

The adversary puts his left forearm under the blow, in such a way blocking your attack. Without releasing his right arm by your right hand, catch his extremity by your left one near the elbow and raise it up. Make the back crossed step forward and take the crossed position. Synchronously with it, strike the direct blow by the right palm in his belly or groin zone (fig.40-42).

The adversary blocks your attack by his left palm. Catch his right arm by both hands and pull him on yourself. The opponent's natural reaction is to try to restore the lost balance by applying a force in the opposite direction. Using the moment and force of the adversary, who tries to snatch his arm back, catch it near the elbow and wrist and overthrow the opponent back, as if rushing following it (fig.43-45).

In this situation the adversary moves his caught right arm round clockwise, transfers your effort aside and crosses his right arm with your right one.

Change places with your opponent and make all exercises of the third track one more time.

39 40 41 42 front view 43 44

45

The fourth track
(Si Lu)

The adversary strikes the direct blow by the right palm forward at the head level. Twist the torso to the right and squat. The left palm is near the right shoulder, the right arm is pulled down towards the left knee. The right leg is pulled to the left one and put on the ground, touching it by the toe. Turn the torso to the right and make the step forward by the right leg. Synchronously with it, catch the adversary's attacking arm and pull it on yourself. Strike the piercing blow forward in the adversary's eyes by fingers of the left hand (fig.46-48).

The adversary has time to put his left shoulder under the blow. Make the step forward by the left leg and turn the torso to the right. You are behind and besides the opponent. After that, strike the double punch by both fists in the adversary's kidney and belly zone (fig.49).

The adversary turns by 180 degrees to the left and makes the step by the right leg towards the turn. Synchronously with it, he takes your attack aside by the left arm. Turn to the right by 360 degrees, make the step by the right leg in the same direction and strike the chopping punch top-down by the back side of the right fist in the adversary's face of breast zone (fig.50, 51).

The adversary blocks your right arm by his left one and prepares to strike the blow by the right arm. Lower your right arm on arc down and release it from the grip. Block his right arm by the left one and take it down. Synchronously strike the blow by the right forearm in the groin from the short distance (fig.52, 53).

The adversary "sticks" his left arm to your right one and presses down and to the left to take your attack to the left from him. Immediately after that, he raises it up. Make the big step forward by the right leg and take both arms apart. Thus, you take his left arm back by your right one and strike the direct blow in his breast by the left palm (fig.54, 55).

The adversary blocks your left arm by his right one. Catch his left arm by your hands and make the "elbow lever" down. At that your right palm presses his elbow top-down (fig.56, 57).

Before you have realized the pain maneuver to the final phase, the adversary knocks your right arm down by his right one, preventing you from pressing his left elbow. Make the step forward by the left leg, turn the torso to the right, pull his caught arm on you. Synchronously with it, press his right elbow by the left forearm bottom-up. At this grip a fracture of the adversary's extremity is possible (fig.58-60).

The adversary presses your left elbow by his left palm, preventing the "elbow lever" up. Turn the torso to the right, take his right arm down by the left hand and strike the ascending punch by the right fist in the chin (fig.61).

The adversary can block your punch by his left palm. Then cross your right arms. You and your opponent are in the initial position.

Now you can make all exercises of this form, having changed places with the opponent.

58   59   60 front view   61

The fifth track
(Wu Lu)

The adversary strikes the direct piercing blow by fingers of the right hand from the initial position. Escaping from this attack, turn through the left shoulder by 180 degrees to the left and make the step by the right leg towards the turn. Take the defending position, raising the left leg, bent in the knee, up and lowering the left arm down. The right arm rises up. At the attack moment catch the adversary's left arm by the right hand, lower the torso down, lower the left leg down and forward and strike the blow by the left palm from yourself in the adversary's belly or groin (fig.62-65).

The adversary blocks your blow by his left arm. Catch his left arm by your right hand, and his right one – by your left hand. Pull the adversary's caught arms by the abrupt movement down and to the right. Strike the biting kick on the opponent's leg by the internal side of the right foot (fig.66).

The adversary tries to push your right arm away by his left one. Lower your right leg on the ground. Make the little step forward and a bit to the left by the left leg. Take your right arm back fast and, having taken the adversary's left arm aside by your left one, strike the direct punch by the right fist in the adversary's belly (fig.67).

The adversary blocks your right arm by his left one. Catch his right arm and pull it on you. The left arm controls the adversary's right elbow. The right knee is put towards the adversary's movement (fig.68).

The adversary steps back by the right leg. He tries to take your right arm away by the left one. Lower the right leg down, make the step forward by the left leg and, having taken the adversary's left arm aside by the left one, strike the side punch by the right fist in the adversary's head zone (fig.69).

The adversary blocks your blow by the left arm. Move your right arm back. Make the step forward by the left leg and substep to it by the right one. Synchronously with it, strike the ascending punch by the right fist in the adversary's chin (fig.70).

The adversary puts his right forearm under your punch. Make the big step forward by the right leg and strike the blow in the throat by the right hand. It is stricken by the spot between the thumb and forefinger of the attacking extremity (fig.71).

The adversary blocks your attack by his left palm. Catch his left wrist by the left hand. Step back by the left leg. Turn the torso to the left. Press the right elbow to the elbow of the adversary's caught arm and make the "elbow lever" down (fig.72).

At the moment when you press your right elbow to the adversary's left arm, he pulls his right arm forward and prevents your maneuver. You are in the position with the crossed arms.

Now you can make all exercises of this form, having changed places with the opponent.

62

63

64

65

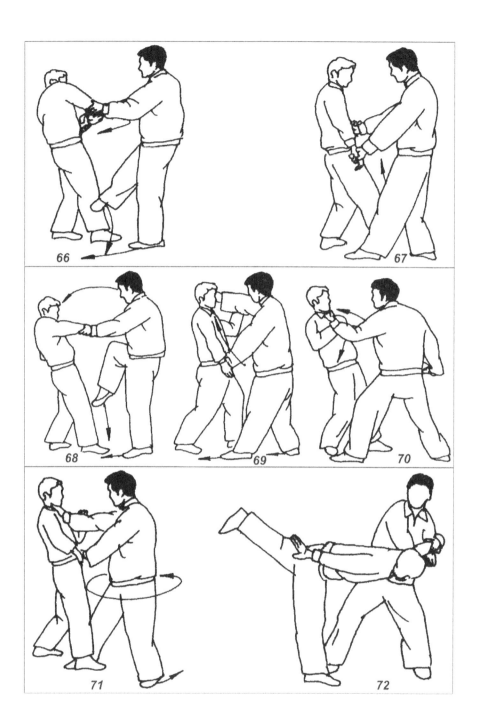

The sixth track
(Liu Lu)

The adversary strikes the direct blow forward by the right arm from the initial position. You lay your right arm on his right one, catch it and pull back and down. Your left arm is laid on his one. Synchronously with it, make the little step forward-to the left by the left leg (fig.73, 74).

The adversary tries to snatch his caught arm back. Use his force and having made the big step by the right leg forward strike the double blow-push in the adversary's breast by the palms (fig.75).

The adversary lays both his palms on your arms and prevents your attack. Make the step forward and to the left by the left leg. Catch the adversary's right arm by the left hand, your right arm remains caught by his left hand. The right arm turns inside and moves forward and up, taking the adversary's left arm back, using the force of the grip of the adversary's left arm. Your left arm takes the opponent's right arm down. The torso a bit turns to the left and both arms synchronously move by the round trajectory abruptly, using the force of the twisting torso (fig.76).

The adversary tries to lower your right arm down by the left one. Following his impulse, bend the right arm and take it to the torso, blocking the adversary's right arm. The left arm controls the opponent's right one near the wrist. Twist the torso to the right and strike the ascending punch by the right fist in the adversary's jaw (fig.77, 78).

The adversary puts his right arm under the punch. Make the little step forward-to the left by the left leg and catch his right arm by your hands. Pull his extremity on you and strike the ascending kick by the right knee in the belly (fig.79, 80).

The adversary lays his left palm on your knee, preventing your attack. Lower the right leg on the ground and strike the ascending blow by the right elbow in the adversary's right side (fig.81).

The adversary steps by the right leg back and blocks your attack by his right arm. Take the adversary's blocking arm away on arc to the left-down by the right arm. Synchronously with it, catch his right arm by the left hand and take it down. Strike the ascending blow in the opponent's chin by the back side of the right wrist (fig.82, 83).

The adversary blocks your blow by his left arm. Raise his left arm up by the left hand. Take you right arm at first to the belly then strike the direct blow by the right palm in the adversary's breast (fig.84).

The adversary pulls his right arm forward and blocks your attack.

You are in the position with the crossed right arms. Now you can make all exercises of this form, having changed places with the opponent.

84

The seventh track
(Qi Lu)

The adversary tries to strike the direct blow by the right arm forward from the initial position. Block his attack by the right arm and catch his right arm. Following its movement, pull it on you. Synchronously with it, make the step forward by the left leg and strike the direct punch by the left fist in the adversary's right side (fig.85, 86).

Using the adversary's strive for taking the caught arm back, make the chasse step forward by the left leg, take his right arm by your left one back and strike the punch by the right fist in the opponent's face (fig.87).

The adversary blocks your attack by his left arm. Catch it by your hands, pull on you and strike the kick by the right foot by his right shin, put forward. After that, turn the torso to the right and strike one more kick by the right foot in his left shin (fig.88, 89).

The adversary knocks your left arm down by his right one, in such a way breaking your grip. Lower your right leg down and make the step forward by the left leg. Raise your arms up, circling the adversary's arms, and strike the coupled blow by the palms in his breast (fig.90, 91).

The adversary lays his palms on your elbows and prevents your attack continuation. Make the step forward-to the left by the left leg, catch the opponent's right arm by both hands and pull it on you. Synchronously with it, strike the strong kick by the right leg in the adversary's right armpit zone (fig.92, 93).

The adversary defends himself from your attack by the left pam. Lower the leg on the ground and make the step to the left by the left leg. Turn by 360 degrees to the right and strike the punch by the back side of the right fist in the opponent's side or spine (fig.94, 95).

He blocks this attack by the right arm. Pull your right leg back and catch his right arm by both hands. Your left hand retains his wrist and presses down. Your right hand catches his elbow and presses up. Thus, you make the pain maneuver "elbow lever" up (fig.96).

The adversary pushes your right arm away by the left one. Make the little step forward by the right leg. Then make the big step forward and to the left by the left leg. Synchronously with it, your right arm rises up on arc, and your left one pulls to the left and down. Your trunk turns to the left, and you try to overthrow the opponent down-to the left on the ground (fig.97, 98).

The adversary releases your right arm by his left hand. He moves his left arm on the round trajectory to the right-down-to the left-up. Your right arms are crossed, and you take the initial position. Now you can make all exercises of this form, having changed places with the opponent.

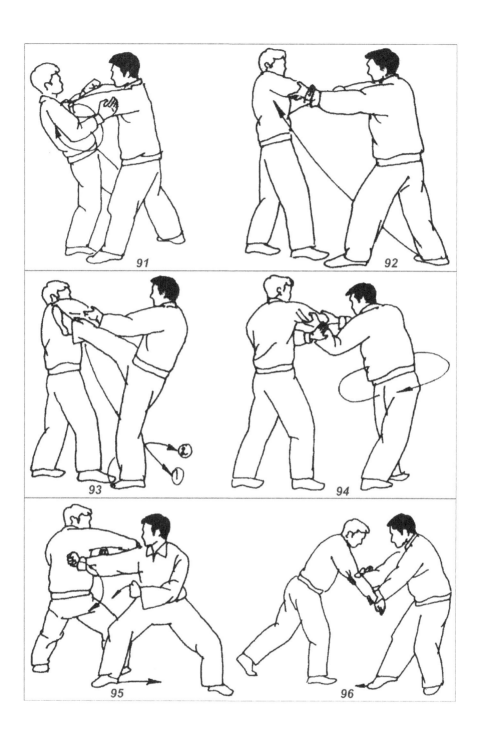

97   98

The eighth track
(Ba Lu)

The adversary strikes the direct blow by the right arm forward from the initial position. Take it away by the right arm, catch the extremity and pull it on you and down. Synchronously with it, strike the direct piercing blow by fingers of the left hand in the face. This blow is blocked by the adversary's left arm. Knock it down by your left arm and, having made the step forward by the right leg, strike the piercing blow by fingers of the right hand in the face. The adversary blocks it by his right palm (fig.99-101).

Catch the adversary's right arm by both hands and pull it on you and down, getting the adversary out of balance. Its natural reaction is to return back. Following him, move your arms up and forward, trying to overturn him back (fig.102, 103).

The adversary knocks your right arm down by his left palm. Make the step forward by the left leg. Strike the round blow in the head by the back side of your right hand (fig.104, 105).

The adversary defends himself from your attack by his right palm. Knock his blocking arm down by the left one and strike one more side blow on his neck by the right palm. Synchronously with it, raise your right leg, bent in the knee, up, defending the lower part of your body from a possible counterattack (fig.106).

The adversary blocks your attack by the left palm. Lower your right leg back to the left. The left arm is taken aside. The right arm moves at first to the breast then it strikes the blow by the palm rib on the adversary's throat (fig.107).

The opponent blocks this blow by the left arm too, after that he counterattacks by the right one. Turn by 360 degrees to the left, knock the adversary's right arm to the external side by the left one, then strike the chopping blow by the right palm rib top-down on his neck or collarbone (fig.108, 109).

The adversary blocks your attack by his left arm. Catch his left arm by your left hand and take it back up to the stop. Make the big step forward by the left leg. Synchronously with it, strike the direct blow by the left palm in the opponent's breast (fig.110).

The adversary blocks this blow by his right arm. After that you cross your right arms and take the initial position. Now you can make all exercises of this form, having changed places with the opponent.

After you are in the position with the crossed arms again, put the right legs back and lower the arms by the sides down (fig.111, 112).

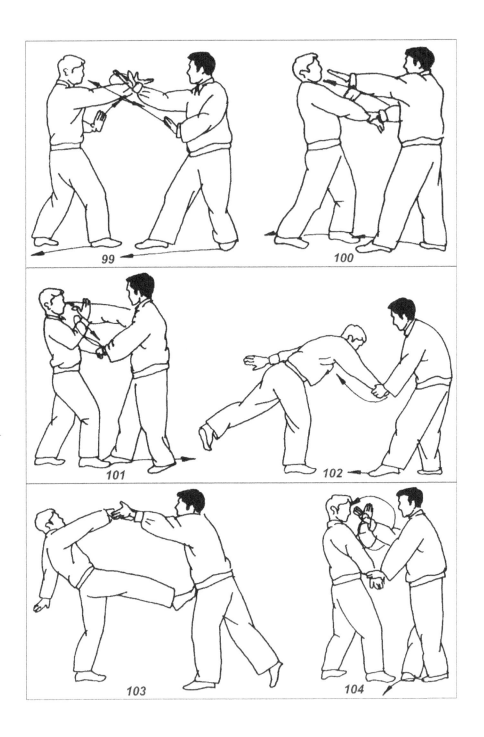

105

106

107

108

109

110

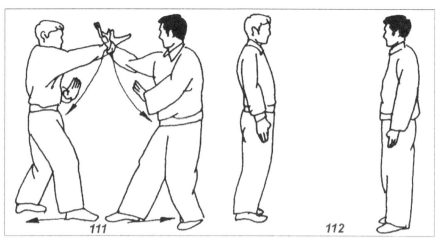

The form is finished

Chapter 7
Bagua Chin-na

At a combat, Baguazhang fighters often use grips, pain maneuvers and different overturns. The whole technical arsenal of **Bagua Chin-na** is divided in three sections.

There are eight small techniques, eight middle ones and eight big ones.

Eight small techniques are called "Dead arm" techniques. The "dead arm" means that an adversary has caught you, so his arm doesn't already move. It is the most comfortable moment for using Chin-na.

Eight middle techniques are more difficult for execution, because they are used, when adversary's arms are "alive" yet. It means that his arms move, for example, an adversary strikes a blow by a fist, and a practicing person catches it and uses Chin-na for beginning "controlling" an adversary.

Eight big techniques are when a practicing person uses Chin-na maneuvers for an attack.

Let's consider main techniques of Chin-na, most often used in Baguazhang practice.

The turning the arm behind the spine

The adversary strikes the direct punch by the right fist. You block it by your left arm and presses the opponent's arm down and inside. Synchronously with it, make the step forward by the left leg, and strike the blow in the groin by the right arm. The adversary must defend himself by the left arm.

Strike the blow by the right arm on the zone of the opponent's right elbow bottom-up. It forces the opponent's arm to bend in the elbow. Then turn to the right and move your right arm above the adversary's one and catch his trapezoidal muscle by fingers.

Now you are pressing on the shoulder by one arm, and on the adversary's hand – by the other, taking it behind the spine. Making this effect, you can force the adversary to fall on the ground. After that, you can start to control him (fig.1-4).

The throw with the grip of the arm on the shoulder

The adversary strikes the direct punch by the right fist in the head. Make the step forward by the left leg, block the opponent's arm from the external side by your right arm and catch its wrist.

Synchronously with it, strike the blow by your left arm in the adversary's breast, belly or chin. Then catch the adversary's shoulder by your left hand and make the step by the right leg on arc back, turning your spine to him.

Bend the torso down, move the pelvis back and make the throw through the shoulder. This technique can be unsuccessful, if you don't block the adversary's right shoulder-blade by your left elbow (fig.5-8).

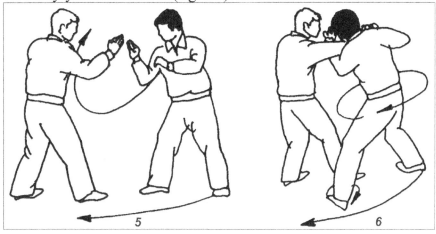

The blocking of the shoulder and elbow

The adversary strikes the punch by the right fist. Make the step by the left leg forward and aside and block the opponent's attack.

Catch the wrist of the adversary's attacking arm by your right hand and make the step forward by the right leg. Go behind the adversary's spine and pull his arm down. It results in blocking the shoulder and elbow that, in its turn, causes the acute pain. The technique may be finished by a throw over the hip (fig.9-12).

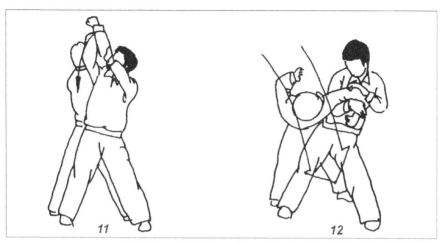

The elbow lever up

The adversary strikes the punch by the right fist in the head. Make the step forward by the left leg, turning to the right, and strike the blow by the right arm on the opponent's elbow. Catch the adversary's wrist by the right hand, and press his elbow bottom-up by the left one. Two arms act synchronously: the left arm presses up, the right one pulls down. Such action blocks the adversary's elbow joint (fig.13, 14).

To seize the elbow

The adversary strikes the punch by the right fist. Make the step to the left, avoiding the attack, and make the block by the right arm, after which catch the opponent's wrist. Synchronously with it, strike the blow by the left arm in the adversary's breast or belly.

Then seize the adversary's right arm by your left one from below. Your arms act synchronously: the right arm presses down, the left arm presses up by the shoulder. The coordinated pressure up and down forces the adversary to straighten, at that his elbow joint is directed up.

Make the step by the left leg in such a way that it is in front of the opponent's right one. After that turn to the right, a bit squat and turn the torso down. Throw the adversary over the left leg and begin to control him (fig.15-18).

15   16

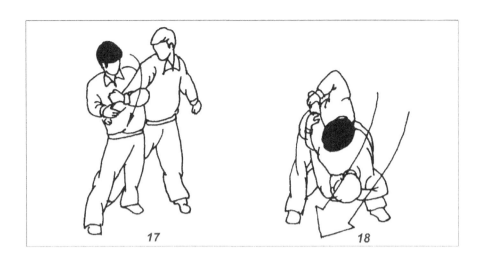

17 18

The elbow lever

The adversary strikes the punch by the right fist in the head. You strike him on the internal side of his arm by your right arm, directing it from you. At that, bend the arm in such a way that helps to defend your head, if the adversary strikes the punch by the left fist.

Synchronously with it, make the step by the left leg in such a way that it is between the adversary's legs, attack the opponent's elbow by the left forearm with a force, turning it. Catch the adversary's forearm by your right hand and press his arm to your collarbone, in such a way blocking his elbow.

Now turn to the right fast, straightening the left leg and keeping the adversary's forearm on your shoulder. Bend forward and press your left elbow on the hollow on the back surface of the opponent's right collarbone (fig.19, 20).

The twisting of the arms

The adversary attacks the head by his right fist. Make the step by the left leg forward and aside, avoiding the attack. Make the block by the right arm and catch the opponent's wrist. Synchronously with it, strike the blow in the adversary's head by your left arm.

The opponent must defend himself, using his left arm. Catch his left wrist by the left hand. Make the step forward by the right leg and turn the torso to the left. At turning pull the adversary's left arm on you and down and his right arm forward from you and down. Overthrow the adversary on the ground (fig.21-24).

The hook from outside

The adversary strikes the punch by the right fist in the head. Make the step aside by the left leg, make the block by the right arm from the external side and catch the wrist of the opponent's attacking arm. Synchronously with it, strike the blow in the head by your left arm. The adversary must defend himself by the left arm.

As soon as the opponent made the block, immediately catch his wrist by your left hand and pull on you and down. The pulling movement is accompanied by twisting the arm along its axis. Your right arm helps it, affecting the adversary's left elbow by the forearm.

Turn the torso to the left, continuing to pull the opponent's arm and hook his right leg by your left one. The adversary is overthrown on the ground. After that you can begin to control him on the ground (fig.25-27).

The big grapevine

The adversary catches your wrist. Press his hand to your right arm by the left palm. The thumb is on the point "Tiger's jaw", and other fingers are placed around the adversary's little finger. Now make the step forward by the right leg and turn to the left.

Bend your right arm in the elbow and lay it above the opponent's arm. Pull your arm on you and aside, synchronously pressing the adversary's forearm. At the same time your left hand and right elbow use the force in the opposite directions. It forces the adversary's wrist to turn inside (the little finger is directed up), its shoulder twists outside, and the elbow bends. The adversary is completely immobilized and blocked (fig.28-30).

28

29

30

The little grapevine

The adversary catches your right hand by his right one. Press his hand to your right wrist by the left palm.

Make the step aside by the left leg and turn to the right. Raise the right hand and pull the adversary's arm on you. At the same time press the adversary's elbow by your left elbow. Now catch the adversary's wrist by fingers of the right hand. A bit squat and turn to the left. It forces the adversary's wrist to turn inside, the elbow – to bend, the shoulder – to turn outside.

Press the adversary's middle carpal joint between the wrist bones and elbow one by the right palm rib, twisting the wrist towards your left leg (fig.31-33).

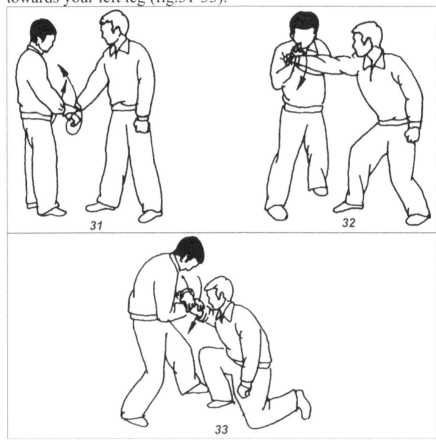

31

32

33

The twisting of the hand outside

The adversary strikes the direct punch by the right fist in the belly. Make the blocking top-down by your left arm and catch the hand of the adversary's attacking arm. Your left thumb presses the back side of his hand. Synchronously strike the blow in the head by your left arm. The adversary must make the block by the left arm.

Begin to twist the opponent's caught hand outside. When his right palm is directed up, catch his hand by your right one. Your arms coordinate their force, the left arm twists outside, the right one presses down, forcing the adversary's wrist to bend outside at an extremely wide angle.

Such effect forces the opponent to fall on the ground (fig.34-36).

34

35

36

The break of the hand

The adversary strikes the direct punch by the right fist in the head. Make the step forward and to the right by the right leg, make the block by the left arm and synchronously strike the direct blow by your right arm in the head. The adversary must block your attack by his left arm.

Catch the opponent's wrist and press it to your right arm. Now use your right forearm, pressing the adversary's hand and bending the wrist back. Synchronously turn the wrist outside. The acute pain forces the adversary to lower on the knees (fig.37-40).

The knock of the leg back

The adversary strikes the direct punch by the right fist in the head. Make the step by the left leg aside. Synchronously with it, knock the opponent's attacking arm down from outside inside by the left palm. Extend your right arm and, having caught adversary's hair or cloth from behind, pull back. Then put the right leg on the back part of the opponent's knee joint and push it down. The movements of the arm and leg must be coordinated for creating the opposite forces and overturn the adversary on the ground (fig.41-43).

41

42

43

Chapter 8
Eight main grips

Baguazhang arsenal includes eight main types of grips that totally form seventy two variants of the use. These maneuvers were collected in a single form for their faster studying. Training these grips, we must remember that their successful application provides the ability to feel an adversary and to follow a situation that is a result of a correct training.

The initial position. You and your partner take the position "A monk holds a cup" and cross your right arms (fig.1).

1. The adversary strikes the blow by the right arm. You block this attack by your right arm and take the attacking arm a bit to the right and down. Catch the opponent's arm by your left hand, knocking it aside and back. Make the step forward by the right leg. Synchronously with it, attack the adversary's throat by the right arm (fig.2, 3).

2. The adversary blocks your attack by his left arm. Bend your right arm in the elbow, controlling the adversary's left arm, then make the step back by the left leg. The torso twists to the left. Catch the adversary's left wrist by your left hand and press his shoulder joint by your right elbow (fig.4-6).

3. The adversary knocks your right elbow down by his right palm. Catch his right wrist and, having put the right elbow to fingers of his right hand, press strongly forward and down, turning his palm back (fig.7-9).

4. The adversary pushes your right elbow away by the left arm. Your right arm goes down, rotates in the elbow joint from the left to the right. Synchronously you press the adversary's wrist to the internal side of your right arm by the left one. Then you abruptly twist his arm counterclockwise. You control his wrist by both arms (fig.10-13).

5. The adversary catches your right wrist by his right hand, in such a way breaking your grip. You put your palm on his wrist, pressing on it from above and from below by the middle finger and thumb and synchronously press his fingers to the right wrist strongly by the left palm. You press the adversary's right wrist by fingers top-down that causes him the acute pain and forces to lower down (fig.14-16).

6. The adversary pushes your left arm away by his left one. Pull his right arm on you. After that take your right elbow to the opponent's left arm, pressing his left wrist between two hands and take the caught arm to the left and back by the jerk, twisting the torso (fig.17-19).

7. The adversary pushes your right elbow away by the right palm and breaks your grip. Make the step back by the right leg, catch his right wrist from above, pressing it between two arms and abruptly twist his right arm around its axis counterclockwise (fig.20-22).

8. The adversary pushes your right elbow, preventing the pain maneuver. Take his right arm by the left arm up then lower your right arm, caught by the opponent, down. After that make the fast movement on arc to the left and down by your left arm. Synchronously with it, raise your right arm on arc to the right and up, in such a way taking your adversary out of balance (fig.23-25).

The final position. The opponent bends his left arm in the elbow and directs the elbow down. Synchronously with it, he moves his right arm on arc down to the left and up. Thus, your right arms are crossed again and you are in the position "A monk holds a cup" (fig.26).

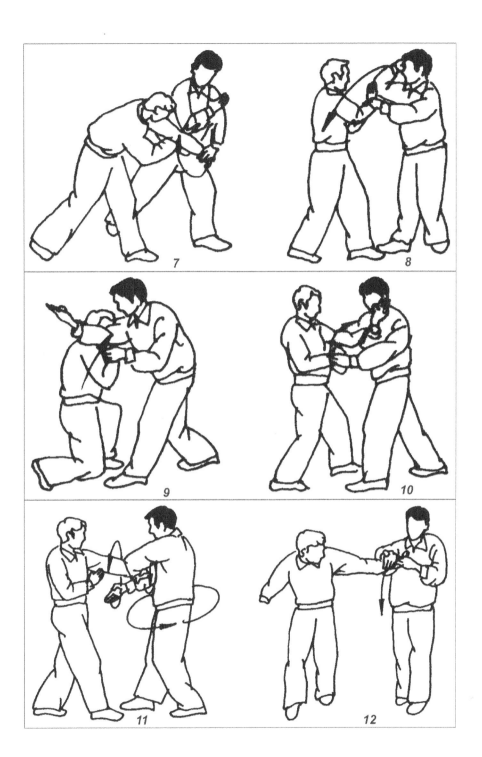

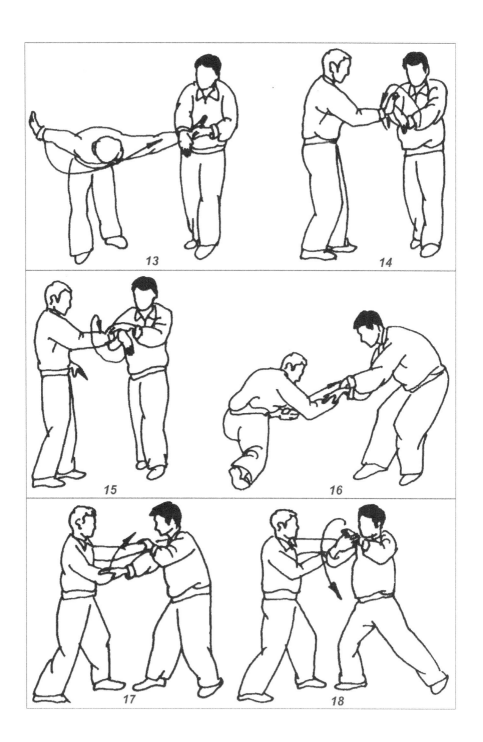

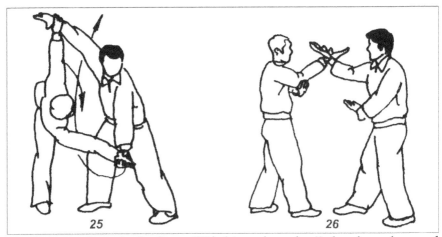

25

26

Repeat the whole form "Eight main grips", having changed places with your partner.

Conclusion

Baguazhang is a rather complicated, wide and at the same time structurally regularized Wushu style, where each "external" movement has its "internal" reason. The technique and traditional Chinese philosophy, considered by Western dwellers as a type of local mysticism, are inseparably interlaced with each other.

This book doesn't pay essential attention to the last aspect, because its volume allows to concentrate only on technical details of the school. Everyone, who wants to become acquainted with Baguazhang theory and philosophy in full, may address to the book of famous **Sun Lutang «Science of the fist of eight trigrams"**, published in all European languages many times.

The author tried to describe the very complicated **Baguazhang style Liang** techniques.

It must be acknowledged, that it is most expedient to study such complicated style as Baguazhang under the guidance of skillful instructors, but the book can replace them, taking into account their deficit.

The aim of this book is to give an idea about **Baguazhang style Liang** and to help to master its special features.

We hope that Baguazhang will help readers not only to improve their health, but also to open possibilities, given to people by such marvelous type of art as **Wushu**, in them.

Made in the USA
Monee, IL
14 September 2023

42742680R00070